MATTERS OF THE HEART

MATTERS OF THE HEART

A Poetry Collection

by *A.B. Dapperens*

Matters of the Heart
A collection of 30 poems by A.B. Dapperens

Copyright © 2015 A.B. Dapperens
ISBN: 978-90-822966-4-8
Paperback edition

Cover Art by Lou Harper - www.louharper.com/Design.html
Proofread by Tami Veldura

First Edition – December 2015

Cayendi Press
Zutphen
The Netherlands
CPress@cayendi.nl

Also available in ebook
ISBN: 978-90-822966-5-5

To Those I love(d)
both lost and found

TABLE OF CONTENTS

DROWNING

loving
it is the sea
the pull of the water
too hard to resist
diving in heart first
regardless
of the fear of slipping under

falling into the black
bottomless abyss
fighting against its hold
yet not wanting to let go
safety within reach
bliss just under the surface

and when the wave has passed
another one is bound to come along

BROTHERS

We are brothers, you and I,
brothers, in all but blood.

We speak the same language,
only needing half a word
to understand the silly jokes
that others never get.

We are brothers, you and I,
brothers, through and through.

I'd go to hell and back for you.
I pick a fight, you clean my mess,
ending up with a bruise or two;
it doesn't matter either way.

Because we're brothers, you and I,
brothers, sworn for life.

MY ENGLISH TEACHER

Thursday, fourth period,
he opens the door and enters.
My eyes are following him,
and my heart surrenders.

For over a year he's been my teacher.
Oh so cute and curly hair.
Though I do not have illusions;
one look at me, he'll see I care.

On his finger a golden ring,
alas... he is not free.
But still he's in my every dream,
and in my dreams he is with me.

All of a sudden my classmate says,
"He's kind of cute, you know?"
I can barely believe she said it;
laughing at her, I almost glow.

For over a year he's been our teacher,
curly hair and oh so cute.
Where has she been all this time,
that only now she understood!

RECIPE FOR LOVE

a hint of a wink
fleeting
almost missed

a free range strut
past you
and then again

has you bracing for
a touch
or a smile

flutter your lashes
shyly
or not so much

to catch him with
a tinge
of desire

just enough to
make him
take you home

COURTING

innocent flirtation
and playful pleasures
with no strings attached

wet kisses
and hurried touches
almost too hot to handle

dark into light
desire turning desperate
sleep is overrated anyway

waking up
to an empty spot
and his number on your chest

HEARTSTRINGS

rhythm pulses through his veins
his heart's counting the beat
his fingers pluck, the strings
creating music from his soul

and somewhere in the background
a girl dances to his tune
under the pretence
he wrote the song for her

alone

JUST ONCE

if only you'd see
me without prejudice
if only you'd let
me see you like
a lover should

if only you'd talk
to me without contempt
if only your touch
were warm
instead of cold

if only... just once
again and again

BROKEN

hearts deranged
estranged

minds unseen
sterile

love brandished
beyond

delicious desire
soothing all

THE END OF THE TUNNEL

heart darkened with despair
fragile trust about to crumble
frantically clawing a way out:
hanging on
to a tiny spark of hope

IS THIS LOVE?

they said the touch
of a soft breeze
on a warm summer's
eve 's what love feels like

when you touched me
my skin burned
my heart raced, and
I forgot all about
what they told me

I don't know if
this is love, but
I never want to
let you go

you

you never caught my eye before
though you stand out in any crowd
I despised you, to be honest
thought you conceited and proud

my view of you was narrow-minded
but your tenacity to reach me strong
you broke through my defences
and I'm pleased you proved me wrong

I was deceived one time too many
it left me bitter and scarred
love had no meaning to me, before
you wormed your way into my heart

I'm not kind nor gentle
yet you accept me as I am
others frown upon our union
but you don't seem to give a damn

you are utterly beautiful
with your smile and boyish charms
and I can conquer anything
when I have you in my arms

BLISS

sweat-slicked bodies
untangling limbs in
catlike stretching
between rumpled sheets

relaxing sighs mixed
with breathless kisses
and heady promises
drifting off...

in silent bliss

MELLOW

whispers of sunlight
skim your body
as you lie beside me
softly snoring

I trace my hand
along your scars
never touching your skin
reluctant to wake you

so you remain asleep
blissfully unaware
giving me longer
to watch you in slumber

INFINITE

love exists
through time
and space

in dreams
as well
as desire

ever-living
never resting
remaining

in infinity

THE TRAGEDY OF WANT

fluttering on the
edge of desire,
body grieving
lack of touch

need turns
into dire fever,
heart bereft
of all delight

anger seeping
through the veins,
the soul cries out:

betrayal

BITTERSWEET VICTORY

you just stand there, smirking
as bittersweet memories flood my mind
the laughter, the secrets we shared
the pain, the trust you destroyed
destroyed me... almost

you once claimed to know me
but you never even bothered
to dig deep enough
now my smile confuses you
I see your confidence falter
now you are but a memory
you have no hold over me...
anymore

THORNS OF LOVE

like a rose
love has its thorns

and leaves
green with envy

like that rose
you prick...

I bleed and
wither

LOVE'S CRY

promised love
between hot tears

a cry forced back into
a breathless laugh

desire
too delicious to end

TO A DANCER

side by side
we move in sync
never quite touching
yet never far
apart

your hand at
my back, guiding
ready to catch me
should I stumble
or fall

you lift me
up high above you;
I feel I could fly
or even touch
the clouds

chest to chest
panting, trembling
you wrap around me
as your warm lips
claim mine

come dance
with me
once more

GIVE AND TAKE — *PART ONE*

To a casual eye it
seems he's merely
leaning on the back of
our sofa—bare chested.

But nothing is that easy.
There's certainly nothing
casual in the way he
grips the pillowed edge.

Neither cries nor tears
mask the fire in his
eyes as he catches
me watching him.

I swallow against my need
to push him further,
but his love remains
as I add another weight.

He wears his pain so
beautifully uninhibited;
a more honest gift
he could not give me.

GIVE AND TAKE — PART TWO

My body screams as I
flex my legs to ease my
strained and burning muscles.

Chains rattle and weights
shift, yet I'm not closer
to any kind of release.

But when I catch his look
through teary eyes, my heart
jumps at his reaction.

To know I caused his hunger
is worth all I suffer
under his control,

until he frees me
from his torture and turns
his pleasure into mine.

WHEN I LOOK AT YOU

Your hair shows me
what the weather is like:
rain or shine,
wind or snow.

When it's too neat,
I want to mess it up.

Your eyes tell me
how you feel today:
sad or mad,
happy or content.

When you wink at me,
I feel wanted.

Your mouth can
scold or invite me,
yet, I like it best with
that hint of a smile
that tells me
you are mine.

And that suits me…
for now.

ONE COIN, TWO SIDES

The sun shone bright
when I was born,
yet darkness lures
along the edge.

I smile, I laugh,
warmed by love,
yet something
feels amiss.

Your absence
casts a shadow,
your dark
absorbs my bright.

My eyes can set
the world alight
when you control
the reins.

One coin, two sides,
one light, one dark,
inside me.

SAYING GOODBYE

with empty hands,
I stand at the
crossroads of my life,
finding it hard to
believe there is happiness
beyond this pain

yet in this endless
nothingness, the
soothing touch of
a memory gives me
the strength to let go
of you in peace,
and pursue my
own path in life

without you

AS THE WORLD TURNS

the sun shines,
grass is green as ever,
but something is empty
inside me

I close my eyes
to catch a glimpse,
but your smile is hidden
forever

the sky is blue
and birds chirp gaily,
but I hear your laughter
no more

the world turns
and stars sparkle
while I grieve your loss,
and miss you

still

BANISHING GHOSTS

shadows
of a long forgotten past
exposed
through the windows of my soul
phantoms
crumbling in the light of spirits
serenity
easing tension, wiping out stress
laughter
finally reclaiming my heart
resonating
like music to my ears

OUT OF PHASE

you weren't quite what I
expected, not even
close to type or gender

but who you are laid claim
to my heart when we met
and everything clicked

we are just out of phase
in a space where we fit
as we are meant to be

the two of us, no labels
just love

COMPLETE

When I met One
my heart soared.
We dined, we talked,
we fell in love
and built a home
together.

Then Two dropped in,
to our surprise.
He filled the space
around, between,
he made us feel
complete.

When Two brought Three,
we weren't keen.
She... though cute,
was not for us,
but she made him
happy.

Now all our rooms
are occupied
with One and me,
and Two and Three,
but whom or where
is never set.

Our life is an
endless dance
of joy and tears,
of need and want,
yet never lacks
of fire.

BOUND IN LOVE

standing side by side
hands entwined
and slightly queasy
ignoring erratic heartbeats

expressing feelings
with renewed passion
repeating vows in
an age-old ritual

in front of friends
and loved ones
confirming what
has always been

cementing the bond
between us
unbreakable and
bound in love

MOVING

Every memory, good or bad,
carefully wrapped and sealed.

One last turn of the key
and the past is left behind,
opening a door to the future.

A new house, a new beginning;
a mind filled with plans
of how to fit it all

to make it feel like home.

ACKNOWLEDGEMENTS

A big thanks to:

My critters—Elin, Jordan, Susan, Tami, and Tim—for helping me iron out the kinks, and making me less nervous about sharing my work.

Lou, for the gorgeous cover art,

Tami Veldura, for the proofreading, and saving my lurk ;)

Val, for help with my bio,

Jarsto, Dorinde, and Jasper, for being there for me, and answering all my strange questions,

My Men, for supporting me. I love you.

ABOUT THE AUTHOR

A.B. Dapperens is a Dutch author who sings her way through life in platform boots and a head filled with clouds of magic, mystery, and fantasy.

Born and raised in Zutphen, the Netherlands, A.B. grew up telling her favourite doll stories to help herself fall asleep, until she discovered writing them was even more fun. While naturally drawn to storytelling, A.B. enjoys the challenge of poetry, of playing with words to create depth and emotion.

Regular meetings with her singing- and wellness coach keep A.B. from disappearing into her own world completely, a feat very much appreciated by her long-suffering husband, sons, and cairn terrier.

Writing as Blaine D. Arden, A.B. won an EPIC Award in 2015 for her short fantasy *"Oren's Right"*, and her scifi romance *"Aliens, Smith and Jones"* received an Honourable Mention in the Best Gay Sci-Fi/Fantasy category of the Rainbow Awards 2012.

A.B. can be found at:
her author page: http://www.cayendi.nl/?page_id=111
email: CPress@cayendi.nl